S0-AJV-769

FAMOUS FIDDLIN' TUNES

BY CRAIG DUNCAN

QWIKGUIDE®

1 2 3 4 5 6 7 8 9 0

Arkansas Traveler

Traditional Hoedown

Back Up and Push

Traditional

The Blarney Pilgrim

Irish Jig

Beaumont Rag

Traditional

Bill Cheatham

Oldtime Hoedown

Billy in the Lowground

Oldtime Hoedown

Blackberry Blossom

Hoedown

Bonaparte's Retreat

Cottoneyed Joe

Texas/Western Version

Cottoneyed Joe

Oldtime/Eastern Version

Cripple Creek

Traditional

Down Yonder

Dill Pickle Rag

Rag - Charles Johnson 1907

D.C. al Fine

Drowsy Maggie

Irish Reel

Durham's Bull

Traditional Hoedown

Eighth of January

Old Time - traditional

Fisher's Hornpipe

Traditional

*optional part

Fire on the Mountain

Old Time-traditional

Garry Owen

Irish/American Jig

Haste to the Wedding

Jig

This page has been
left blank to avoid
awkward page turns

Jolie Blonde

Henry Choates - Cajun Waltz

Maiden's Prayer

Traditional

31

Merrily Kiss the Quaker

Irish American Jig

The Monaghan Jig

Irish Jig

optional part

D.C. last time only

Miss McLeod's Reel

Hop Light Ladies, Did You Ever See the Devil, Uncle Joe

Traditional

Morrison's Jig

Irish Jig

D.C.   last time only

Mississippi Sawyer

Old Time - traditional

Old Joe Clark

Old Time - traditional

Ragtime Annie
Raggedy Ann

Traditional

Red Wing

Kerry Mills

Roxanna Waltz

Traditional Contest Waltz

41

St. Anne's Reel

Traditional

Sally Ann *or* Sail Away Ladies

Oldtime

Sally Goodin

Old Time Traditional

Sally Johnson

Contest - Old time

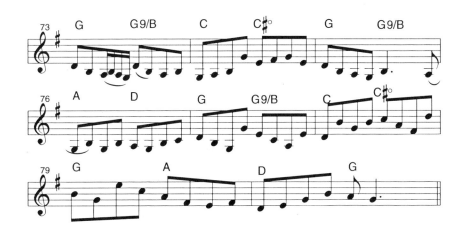

Salt Creek

Old Time-Bluegrass-traditional

Smash the Windows

Jig

Soldier's Joy

Old Time Traditional

Swallowtail Jig

Traditional Jig

Star of the County Down

Traditional Irish

Temperance Reel

Irish Reel

Turkey in the Straw

Traditional

Westphalia Waltz

Waltz - traditional